the complete
SIGH
in Sentences

The Complete Sight Words in Sentences contains the 306 sight words from the original book, plus 301 additional words.

The Complete Sight Words in Sentences contains practice for SnapWords® Lists A-G, Nouns 1 & 2, and Verbs in 400 sentences, color-coded by level.

607 high-frequency words are included: 220 Dolch, 300 Fry, and 500 Fountas & Pinnell, and more.

Use for sight word assessment or fluency practice after student has mastered each list of words using the stylized cards. Also aids in comprehension and correct usage of words in context.

Child1st Publications, LLC

The Complete Sight Words in Sentences
Ages 6 and up.

© 2012 Sarah K Major
Printed in the United States of America

ISBN: 978-1-936981-43-4

Design: Sarah K Major

Published by Child1st Publications, LLC
800-881-0912 (phone)
888-886-1636 (fax)
www.child1st.com

Other titles by Sarah K Major:
Kid-Friendly Computation series: *Addition & Subtraction*, *Place Value*, and *Right-Brained Multiplication & Division*. *The Illustrated Book of Sounds & Their Spelling Patterns*, *Alphabet Tales*, The Easy-for-Me™ Reading Program, and the Easy-for-Me™ Books.
Other educational work: SnapWords® and SnapLetters™.

TABLE OF CONTENTS

ABOUT THIS BOOK

Content:

Sections are color-coded to match SnapWords® Lists A-Verbs colors and symbols. Each section contains only the sight words listed on each section page, with the addition of some number and color words and the following words:

Level A	Level B	Level C	Level D	Level E
ball	book	kids	bikes	bad
cap/caps	cake	pets	door	cars
cat/cats	house	story	friends	park
dad	pizza		river	trip
dog	toys		street	
home			sun	
Mom				

Level F	Level G	Level Nouns 1	Level Nouns 2	Level Verbs
pants	fish	camp	toss	butterfly
pet	trees	tent		
pig				

Suggested uses for *Sight Words in Sentences:*

Independent Practice:	Assessments:	Writing Prompts:
When a child believes he knows a sight word list, let him review the words using this book in a reading center or at home with a parent. Allow him access to the corresponding stylized sight words (SnapWords®*) so he can look up a word he might not remember.	After a child has used this book to check herself, have her ask a partner to listen to her read the section (A, B, C, etc.). Once a student listener has been through the sentences with her, the teacher may use this book to do a final listening assessment.	*Sight Words in Sentences* is great for enhancing comprehension, reinforcing correct word usage, and for writing prompts. Many of the sentences allude to a story that will inspire a child to write and then draw. For instance, in the green section, "I see two up the tree" might inspire your student to describe two monkeys and write about what they are doing in the tree.

*SnapWords® stylized sight words are essentials for teaching high-frequency words to right-brained learners. Words are embedded in images, and the child's brain snaps a picture of the word and stores it in memory complete with its context and meaning. Later, the image is the vehicle for recall. The word is used in a sentence on the reverse of each card, which enhances comprehension and usage. The body motion provided is another avenue for learning and recall, valuable to kinesthetic learners. SnapWords® are comprised of the Dolch list, the Fountas & Pinnell 500 most frequently recurring words, and 300 Fry words, and more. For more information about SnapWords® Cards and to download free trial cards, visit **www.child1st.com**.

SnapWords™ List A:

a	down	it	ran
an	for	jump	said
and	get	like	see
are	go	little	sit
as	has	look	so
at	have	make	stop
back	he	me	the
big	help	my	this
but	here	no	to
by	hi	not	up
call	his	now	want
can	I	on	we
come	if	or	will
did	in	out	you
do	is	play	

You and I are at home.

Are you in the big, blue one?

I will go up but will not come down.

Come and sit by me.

I can not call for help now.

Will you do this for me as you go?

Come down here. Do not go up.

The dog and an orange cat ran.

Stop by at three so we can play.

Do not make me look for you!

No, I did not call, but I ran out!

Come, make a yellow one now.

Four or five will get to go.

I have green, but you have red.

He has a yellow one.

I want help on this!

His dad is back here now!

Can it jump like my little dog?

He has a big, red ball.

He said, "Did you do this?"

I see two or three up here.

Four or five will look for me.

Six will want to go.

I have his seven little cats.

Look out! No one ran.

Come on! We can play now!

I will call to see if he can play.

Mom said, "Do you want to stop?"

Can you see this is not so big?

We ran by the little, white cats.

I said, "Hi. Can I sit down here?"

Look! I can jump like you.

Now we can get out and play.

Two caps are gold and gray.

I want a pink or purple cap.

I want to go up.

Go see if it is in here.

Is it on my little dog?

Hi! Here we are!

We will jump back a little.

SnapWords® List B:

about	good	put	they
all	got	read	too
am	him	run	took
any	into	saw	try
ask	its	say	us
ate	just	she	went
away	last	show	what
be	let	sing	when
cut	many	still	who
eat	may	take	why
fast	must	tell	with
fly	new	than	work
from	of	that	yes
funny	our	them	your
gave	pull	then	

Read and then sing all about it.

Run away fast from the black cat!

Why did you ask for any of
our work?

I just cut the good cake to eat!

I saw that the last one got into
its home.

I just gave him a funny book!

I saw him run to read the new book.

Show me what you put on it.

They took pizza and then ate it all.

Who wants to pull this with us?

I will ask, "What is your work?"

Eight of us went when you called.

He may let many of us fly it, too.

We must put all of our new
toys away.

I still say she will show us ten books.

Tell them to take the toys home.

I am still bigger than you are.

He went away; then they took
nine toys.

I will say why we got into the
brown house!

I got away from the black dog!

We will run fast from the dog!

Try and cut the cake for us to eat!

Yes, I gave him a good pizza!

Let me try to be still just for your last show!

What will you try that is new?

When did you get your new toy?

Who went with them to pull it?

Why did you say yes to them?

I took them home to fly and they will be good here.

Will you be here? I will tell about any funny books I read.

Ask me if you eat that pizza!

You must try the new toy!

My dog will be bigger than my cat.

Many of us may read the new book.

I saw them take its toy.

She can show you that they ate it.

When they went, they took it, too.

I will ask, "May I cut the last good one?

She will sing all about it if I am here.

Dad took them to work with him.

SnapWords® List C:

after	find	long	some
again	first	made	soon
another	found	man	there
around	give	more	these
before	giving	much	think
began	going	never	those
better	gone	next	told
bring	had	off	under
came	hard	oh	very
cold	her	old	walk
day	hold	other	was
didn't	how	over	were
does	kind	own	where
don't	know	pick	which
far	live	ride	

I will run around again after you do.

Go first before you pick
another one.

They came and began to work
this day.

It is a cold day so you had better
bring a cap.

Didn't he give you a toy he found?

Does she find her dog hard to hold?

First I know I must find my mom.

These kids will bring those toys.

How kind of you to think
about giving!

Let us go around one more house.

I don't live very far away; does he?

Which toys were you going
to bring next?

Don't go so far again!

I was going, but he was long gone.

I know how kind the man is!

She made much more than he did!

I will never get her off the next ride!

Oh! Look over there at the
other ride!

I had better not bring some
old pizza!

I was going to call again soon after
she had gone.

We came in; it was cold out there!

Before I began to eat much,
I worked under the house.

Walk under this long one very fast.

He works where the silver ones
are made.

I own some old toys. I want to pick
new ones.

I think these will soon go under.

I told those kids to walk, not ride!

Those kids will walk very fast
over the other one!

Oh! I told you where we were.

Which of you likes what I made?

I think these are all there are now.

Those kids told the man a very long story.

I will give the book I found to him another day.

Oh! Next I will take off my other old cap.

Soon I will own some more pets.

I didn't know how kind the man was!

I know I will never live here before I go over.

I know you will never live around another dog that is hard to hold.

It is never hard for her to hold it.

I am giving her a better ride soon.

Section D

SnapWords® List D:

across	fall	might	sleep
always	full	most	small
animal	goes	myself	start
been	grow	near	their
best	high	need	today
both	hot	once	turn
buy	hurt	only	upon
clean	I'm	open	use
close	keep	pretty	warm
could	laugh	right	well
done	leave	round	while
draw	left	same	would
even	light	short	yet
every	mean	should	

I will go across the full river today.

We have always been best friends.

Both of us could close the door.

Draw every one, and I will even laugh!

It will start small but will grow full and high.

Keep the books when you are done.

I have always been the best at play!

I might get hurt if I fall upon the street when I turn.

Both of them will use their new bikes.

I could have done that well, too!

You should not be mean to your friend.

Start small, then let it grow high up!

I'm hot so I might need to leave.

Most of the light had left the fall day.

I need you to not be mean near me!

It is all right to only open it once.

All six animals are the same: pretty, short, and round.

All ten should start their work the same day.

It is their turn to buy a new, clean ball today.

Six small cats could use all of that.

I am always warm while I work.

I have even done the most work
by myself.

Will the short one fall and get hurt
while you sleep?

It is pretty, light, and goes
left and right well.

I'm warm when I'm upon the
house.

It is your turn to use the bike, but don't keep it.

It always goes well while you are around.

Would you want to leave yet?

He asked if I would go across by myself yet.

I should clean up before I sleep!

Should you buy that small, round one?

Once you open it, it will not be the same.

I might draw one for my best friends.

I am too hot to turn every one over.

I will only say this once: close the door!

Are you done with that book yet?

The best animal is clean, pretty, and near me.

He should sleep a short while today.

She always goes across every river.

The full sun is high and hot.

Section E

SnapWords® List E:

accident	enough	passenger	thought
basement	father	playmate	through
because	flapping	pleasant	together
bicycle	giggle	please	tomorrow
breath	heard	pleasure	toward
careful	hitch	prize	twice
carry	hundred	realized	wash
certainly	husband	shall	whole
clapped	imagine	stove	willing
company	indeed	struggled	wish
decide	instant	stuck	wonderful
different	it's	stumbled	write
drink	mother	thank	

They had an accident in our basement twice!

I was careful to carry them because they were full.

Mother, he certainly does have bad breath!

Our company clapped when I was on my bicycle.

I can not decide what is different about this drink!

I heard eight kids giggle, and that was enough!

The passenger and I had a pleasant trip together.

Please hitch a hundred cars together tomorrow.

I certainly can not decide which one to drink!

I wish you were willing to wash your whole bicycle!

I imagine it's very pleasant in the basement now!

I realized he was careful to carry them to the stove.

The husband thought he heard the hitch flapping.

I imagine we must have a hundred books now!

The passenger needs a playmate this instant!

It was a pleasure to give the dog its prize.

I realized it was pleasant as I went toward the park.

Father struggled to get the stove in the house. It got stuck.

That company got the prize because it's wonderful indeed.

She stumbled through the door and got stuck right after.

They struggled to read the whole book together twice.

Tomorrow we can make a different instant drink for Mother.

Her husband imagined he heard a big accident.

He said, "Yes, indeed. There was an accident!"

We all stumbled toward home together.

We thought we would go through the park.

I got stuck twice as I went toward the house.

I shall write to thank my wonderful father and mother.

Tomorrow I shall be willing to write it twice.

I wish you were willing to wash the whole stove.

Mother and Father think I'm wonderful, thank you!

I certainly will keep you company with pleasure.

Please! Eight different dogs is enough!

I shall be with you in an instant!

They start flapping because she giggles.

We thought it through together.

I realized I shall indeed get the prize.

I thought we could go through there.

We will go toward home tomorrow.

I am willing to wash the whole
house twice.

Section F

SnapWords® List F:

along	end		set
also	face	money	sister
anything	fat	morning	someone
bed	fine	name	something
box	hand	night	special
car	happy	o'clock	stand
cat	hat	order	store
coat	home	pair	such
color	hope	part	thing
dear	later	present	third
dog	letter	push	though
door	longer	room	until
dress	love	sat	way
each	maybe	second	yesterday
early	men	seem	yours

I hope my present is a new coat and hat.

Maybe I will write a longer letter later.

My sister wants to come along, also.

That special present is yours; I see your name on it.

There is not anything in the box under my bed.

My new coat, hat, and dress are the same color.

The men worked for money from morning until night.

There is no such thing as a happy car.

My dear dog and cat think they are something special!

It's fine with me if you order a pair from the store.

I love going home at the end
of each day.

Part of them sat, and part of them
will stand until the end.

Put a red door on the second
room and a blue one on the third.

Someone will push his way out
of the room.

You seem to be happy today, even
though yesterday you were not.

My pet pig has a fat face, even though he is still little.

On your way to the store, will you set the box in the car?

My coat, hat, and dress are all a pretty color.

You look happy, even though the present is not yours!

Will you push the box under the bed or into the next room?

I hope you give me a hand as
I push this box.

My little sister is someone special
to me.

Each of us left something
at home.

I am fine with anything, even
though that is *not* special!

Later, maybe, we can order more
of these.

My part of the present is that red thing.

I got a pair of pants at the store yesterday.

She sat in the room longer than he did.

Maybe we can end this early in the morning.

My dog got in my face! He is such a dear!

I will write the letter later, maybe
at three o'clock!

The men who stand that way
seem happy.

Hand me the money
by two o'clock.

You are first, he is second,
and she is third.

If you have the same name,
maybe you have the same home.

I will name my black dog "Night" and my yellow cat "Morning.

Yesterday the men made a lot of money at work.

My sister will come along with us also.

I would love to order a set of those.

This part of the work can sit here until later.

Section G

SnapWords® List G:

able	deep	heavy	ready
above	dry	important	real
against	during	inside	really
almost	easy	instead	scared
already	either	large	several
although	else	less	sick
among	ever	lot (lots)	side
bad	favorite	mad	simple
beautiful	few	main	since
behind	finally	nice	size
below	free	often	sound
between	front	page	sure
brother	fun	perhaps	that's
certain	great	possible	themselves
dark	half	probably	they're
		quick	top

Are you able to carry the heavy box to the top?

I am against going into a deep, dark well!

You are already almost ready to go!

She ran between my brother and me.

There is a certain page that is my favorite.

Perhaps they're finally nice
and dry.

Mom said she will probably be
ready really soon.

He went below, but I will probably
go inside instead.

It was easy to run, although
I got behind!

My brother and I are inside.
I am above; he is below.

A few of us stand between the trees and several don't.

They often have fun by themselves. That's great!

Half of them are size large; a few are my favorite!

The important man sat in front during the main part.

A few among us can only play a simple sound.

He has been really sick since he ate some bad pizza!

You either make your bed, or else no play!

I made my bed and finally was free to go play!

Are you ever sure which side you are against?

I took a quick look to see if it was real, although I was scared!

It is possible Mom will not be mad at either of us.

Eat less of that and lots of this instead!

They often like to turn the page for themselves.

They're at the top among all of us.

I already said I am almost inside. Perhaps you will come in, too?

Finally we found some real, nice ones!

Half the fish are nice and large. That's great!

Since I got sick, I'm not sure I like the sound of that to eat!

It is important to be as quick as possible.

Several kids were scared of the size of the large men.

During the day it is really easy to not be scared.

My brother said there is a deep, dark, dry well between the trees.

She put the small ones in front and the large ones behind.

I am not able to pick that up; it is too heavy!

Please give me less, not a lot! It is not my favorite.

I don't ever eat anything else,
just a lot of this!

The main thing that made me mad
was so simple.

I'm sure he will pick me to be
on his side.

I'm certain she put the beautiful
ones above, not below.

I'm finally free to go play and
have fun!

SnapWords® Nouns1:

ball		people	stick
bird	flower	planet	storm
book	food	plant	street
boy	friend	rain	sun
chair	giant	river	table
children	girl	rock	teacher
city	grass	sand	town
clothes	hair	school	tree
cloud	head	shirt	water
country	house	shoe	wind
crab	insect	sign	woman
desk	island	snake	words
ears	lizard	snow	world
eyes	ocean	spider	worm
fire	paper	stake	year

The children have a bird book and a ball to play with.

The giant has big ears and eyes on his giant head.

The giant has big clothes, big hair, and a big chair.

His house is on an island out in the ocean.

There is a tree on his island and water all around.

In a storm, the rain falls on the tree, into the river, and on the ocean.

The sun goes behind a cloud, and the wind is cold.

A boy went from the country to the city to buy food.

In the city he saw many people on the street.

At the store, he saw a woman and a girl with red hair on her head.

The sign at the store had red words that said, "Get a crab today."

So the boy got a crab to put on the fire at his house.

The children went to school in town. They took paper with them.

The teacher sat on a chair at a desk with some paper and a book.

Her book had really big words on each page.

The book was about a lizard
on a rock.

There was also a spider on a stick
in the sand.

Soon a worm and an insect got off
the stick and got on the plant.

They wanted to eat the plant and
the flower, too.

But then a snake ate the spider and
the insect!

I want to camp in the country with my friend this year.

Our tent has a stake to hold it up in the grass.

We like to read about the world and another planet, too.

We read that the world has water like oceans and rivers.

It has islands, sand, and rocks.

Our planet has wind, sun, snow, rain, and storms.

It has flowers, birds, insects, lizards, snakes, and spiders.

In a country you can find a town and a city with many streets.

The boy and girl live in a great big house with other people.

This year they will plant grass and a flower.

The boy had a red shirt for school and a blue shirt for home.

He had one shoe on the day before school began.

He thought the teacher would not like only one shoe.

So the boy took off the first shoe. He went to school with no shoes.

At school, the teacher had shoes on a table. She got a pair for the boy.

Then the boy found his shoe so he took the pair back to school.

At school he saw other children who didn't have shoes.

The teacher gave them shoes and shirts from her table.

Then all the children sat down at their desks to read.

All the children read books about the planets. It was great!

Section Nouns2

SnapWords® Nouns2:

air	feet		sea
baby	field	line	ship
bike	fish	list	sky
boat	game	Mom	space
body	group	moon	spring
boot	heart	nothing	state
bus	hill	number	story
class	hour	park	stuff
dinner	idea	party	summer
Dad	job	past	things
dream	kids	person	time
earth	lady	picture	trouble
fact	land	place	week
family	lunch	problem	winter
fare	life	reason	yard

My dream is to ride my bike with my family this summer.

Mom and Dad say it is good for my heart and body to ride.

After dinner, we ride in a field and up a hill for an hour.

Another day, Dad, Mom and I went up a hill on our bikes.

In fact, in the summer, we like to fish on the sea in our boat.

The air is hot and the sky is blue as we toss our lines into the sea.

I had trouble with my line, but in a short time, Mom had a fish!

As we ate lunch in the boat on the sea, we saw a large ship go past.

After lunch, fish began to spring into our boat at one time!

Our family has a new baby. Now we have two kids!

I love this baby with all my heart! I play with her for an hour.

Mom and Dad like it when I play a game with baby at the park.

The reason my feet are large and her feet are not is that she is a baby.

In winter, the air is cold and we play games in the snow.

I have boots for my feet for winter. Nothing gets inside my boots.

I read a story by the fire. My favorite picture is of the moon.

I had an idea for a game to play in the yard, in the winter.

One time in a dream I had trouble with one person in our group.

That person did not want to pay the fare for the bus ride.

In my dream, I gave him the fare and also my place on the bus!

The lunch lady has a job for an hour to give the kids fish.

One person in our group said, "I have a real problem with fish."

The lunch lady said, "Fish is good for your heart and your body."

Our class got in line and went to play in the field for an hour.

In class, we read about the earth, space, and life on land.

The moon is in space, and air is in the sky around the earth.

All of life is on land, in the sea, and in the sky.

The earth has hills, fields, seas, kids, and animals.

The reason I like class is that I like to read about this stuff.

In the past, people thought the earth was not round.

Next week our class will go on the bus to another state.

The fare for the bus ride to the other state is $5.00 for each person.

We made a list of things to bring so nothing is left out.

My idea is to have a party in the park next week. I can picture it!

I have trouble with a number of things at my place.

The problem is they don't have a place of their own.

When you clean a ship, nothing helps more than a list of jobs to do.

In fact, the lady likes to stuff us at dinner and then read a story.

After dinner, a number of fish began to spring into our boat!

Every summer we have a dinner party in our yard.

SnapWords® Verbs:

add	couldn't		stay
answer	died		stood
became	explain	knew	study
become	feel	learn	succeed
begin	fell	listen	talk
being	fight	lost	teach
believe	finish	mind	throw
broke	fix	miss	travel
brought	follow	move	tried
build	forget	organize	understand
can't	form	quit	wasn't
care	grade	rest	watch
catch	hear	seen	win
caught	hit	shot	woke
change	kept	speak	worry
complete	killed	spend	wouldn't

I believe I can answer when I begin to add four numbers!

When you explain, I do care if I can't catch on.

Our grade stood in two lines, and it was a fight to the finish!

I knew that broke. Follow me and I will teach you to fix it.

I tried to understand when you explained the problem.

Hear this: I feel we need a complete change here!

I knew I couldn't change their minds.

I wouldn't mind if we don't organize this stuff!

I woke up with a worry that I wouldn't finish in time.

I want to watch you win, so don't quit until you succeed.

The worm lost its coat and became a beautiful butterfly.

Stay and spend the day; I will miss you when you move!

If I listen, I will learn and understand when you teach me.

The lady will talk about how to study so you can succeed.

He brought the rest of the things so we can begin to build.

I forget which one he kept; it's possible it's at his house.

He will throw the ball; I hope I succeed when I try to hit it.

I will stay here and rest after I travel and after I speak.

I become scared when I see a giant animal!

I have seen Bob make one great shot after another!

On this form, I tried to add up the numbers, and I am being careful.

Please follow me before you forget how to fix this.

Mom will speak: "Learn to listen so you don't get lost."

I'm willing to take a shot at being organized. I hope I catch on!

I worry that I can't win. Maybe I will spend the day and study.

I hear he hit the ball one time in my yard and then fell over.

If you move this, I will miss it when I travel.

I stood to talk about how I travel over the sea to another country.

He woke up and said he wasn't going to care if you get the answer!

I feel I really can't become a part of this fight.

I caught a bug, but Mom said I couldn't keep it.

If I put the bug I caught into a box it would have died!

I let the bug go, but then I fell on it and killed it by accident!

I have seen him throw the ball, and it wasn't bad at all!

We have seen how men build a tall house.

I watch and try to understand how you became lost!

You can't worry about how the teacher will grade the form.

If I will complete the job, that means I will finish it.

I couldn't believe he brought the things he broke!

I have seen her organize all her stuff and not quit!

COMPATIBLE PRODUCTS

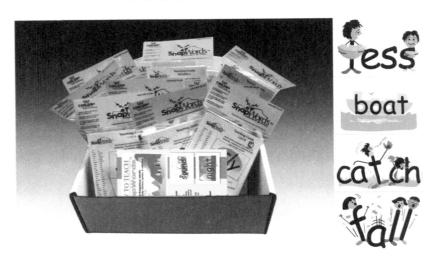

607 SnapWords® Cards

SnapWords® picture sight words are essentials in helping visual learners and young children learn to read more easily. Using picture sight words will make an immediate difference for new or struggling learners. You may successfully teach our Dolch sight words to children of any age. We currently have 607 picture sight words, including Lists A-G, Numbers & Colors, Verbs, Nouns List 1, and Nouns List 2. Get them today and help your child love learning.

Follow this link to purchase:

http://www.child1st.com/miva/merchant.
mvc?Screen=CTGY&Store_Code=CPL&Category_Code=SW

Or simply search for "Child1st 607 SnapWords Teaching Cards."

ABOUT CHILD1ST PUBLICATIONS

Core Beliefs:

We believe every child can learn, that many learning failures are avoidable, and that a label assigned doesn't have to be a life sentence. We believe brains are made to learn, they love to learn, and in most cases they will learn when conditions are right. We also believe that once the gaps in their understanding are bridged, children will progress rapidly.

Product designers at Child1st look at children first to discover how they learn most naturally. We integrate explicit phonics instruction with specific strategies (visuals, movement, storytelling, humor, rhyme, and patterns) to engage children with an array of learning strengths. Teach smarter, more efficiently, and with confidence.

Background:

After many years teaching everything from preschool to college and developing products along the way to meet observed needs, Sarah Major resigned from fulltime teaching in 2006 in order to devote herself to Child1st. What began as a small business in her Florida home quickly grew, gaining friends and customers all over the world. By 2008 the business expanded to a new facility and added several staff.

Contact Us:

Web: www.child1st.com
Phone: 800-881-0912

CPSIA information can be obtained at www.ICGtesting.com
Printed in the USA
BVOW10s2202250115

384574BV00011B/10/P